LET'S VISIT PERU

Let's visit
PERU

GARRY LYLE

First published 1985
© Garry Lyle 1985

ACKNOWLEDGEMENTS

The Author and Publishers are grateful to the following organizations and individuals for permission to reproduce copyright photographs in this book:
Mike Howarth, Eugénie Peter, Christopher Stone, Travel Photo International and Photothèque Vautier-de Nanxe.

DEDICATION

The Publishers take pride in dedicating this book to the memory
of Garry Lyle who, sadly, died before it was printed.

Lyle, Garry
  Let's visit Peru
  1. Peru – Social life and customs – Juvenile literature
  I. Title
  985'.0663   F3410
ISBN 0 222 00952 7

Burke Publishing Company Limited
Pegasus House, 116-120 Golden Lane, London EC1Y 0TL, England.
Burke Publishing (Canada) Limited
Registered Office: 20 Queen Street West, Suite 3000, Box 30, Toronto, Canada M5H 1V5.
Burke Publishing Company Inc.
Registered Office: 333 State Street, PO Box 1740, Bridgeport, Connecticut 06601, U.S.A.
Filmset in Baskerville by Graphiti (Hull) Ltd., Hull, England.
Printed in Singapore by Tien Wah Press (Pte.) Ltd.

Contents

	Page
Map	6
Mountain Sandwich	7
Before the Spaniards	21
Conquerors and Colonists	31
The Independent Republic	41
Earning a Living	53
Coast and Capital	61
The High Central Region	72
Under the "Eyebrow"	86
Peru in the World	91
Index	94

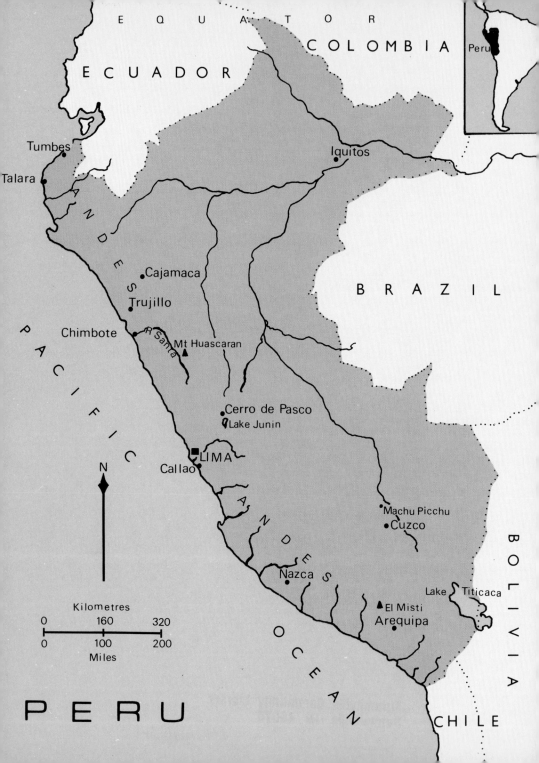

Mountain Sandwich

Peru is one of the few countries where you can travel more than 2,300 kilometres (1,400 miles) north and south without noticing any large change in the natural landscape—but you must keep moving either north or south to do this. On the much shorter distances east and west, the changes are great and dramatic. Eastward from the sea, stony and sandy coastlands rise sharply to steep and massive snow-capped mountains—many of them volcanoes—and the mountains drop inland to country as wet and green as the coastlands are brownish and dry.

The mountains are the Andes, which rise higher than any other range in the world except those of central Asia. They cover the whole central length of Peru, and are sandwiched between the 2,300-kilometre strip of almost rainless desert to the west, and the even longer strip of hot, wet tropical forest to the east.

Those strips of desert, mountain and jungled rain forest are the three regions into which Peru is naturally divided. They lie on the western side of South America, between the Equator and the Tropic of Capricorn, and together they give Peru an area of 1,285,000 square kilometres (about 500,000 square miles). That makes Peru a larger country than any of its neighbours except Brazil, and the largest of all the South American countries, except Brazil and Argentina.

A farmstead in the province of Cuzco, with the snow-capped mountains of the Andes towering in the background

Peru's three natural regions have Spanish names. They are called La Costa (the coastlands), La Sierra (the highlands) and La Montaña or La Selva (the woodlands). The names are Spanish because the first Europeans to explore and settle this part of South America came from Spain, and Spanish is still the country's main official language. However, only about half of the nineteen million people who live in Peru today have any Spanish blood. Nearly all the others are full-blooded South American Indians, and two of their Indian languages—Quechua and Aymará—are also official languages in modern Peru.

Most of the full-blooded Indians live in the Sierra region,

where their ancestors were living when the first Europeans arrived in Peru about four hundred and fifty years ago. These highlands are mainly a region of deep, steep-sided valleys winding between peaks that rise as high as 6,768 metres (22,190 feet), but there are also wide and fertile upland basins, and in the south the mountains spread apart round a vast high plain.

Called the Altiplano, which actually means "high plain", this bleak and windy stretch of grassland is itself higher than many of the Alpine peaks in Europe. It surrounds the highest large lake in the world—a lake so large that some of the towns on its shores are linked by steamship services. This is the famous Lake Titicaca, whose waters are shared between Peru and its neighbour Bolivia.

Lake Titicaca is not only a very large lake. It is also a very deep one and, because of its depth, its water is much warmer than might be expected of a lake 3,800 metres (12,500 feet) above sea-level. That in turn makes the air and the land near the lake a good deal warmer than they are on the rest of the Altiplano. This allows farmers in the area to grow barley, maize and several other grain crops, as well as very good potatoes.

In other parts of the Altiplano, crop-farming is not so easy. With an average yearly temperature as low as 4 degrees Centigrade (39 degrees Fahrenheit), the soil will grow very little except coarse pasture grasses, so most of the farming people raise animals rather than grain and vegetables. The animals are sheep, llamas and alpacas (a kind of llama with long woolly hair), all raised for their wool and for meat. Cattle are very rarely

Quechua Indian children in a small village in the Sierra. The Quechua people have lived in this area for many hundreds of years

seen in this part of the Sierra. The climate is too cold for them, and the pasture too thin.

Over the rest of the highland region, conditions vary with the height. Above about 4,200 metres (13,800 feet) even coarse grasses do not grow. At this height, too, some people find it difficult to work; but Indian miners can work on mountainsides up to 1,000 metres (3,280 feet) higher without being much upset by the mountain sickness which troubles Europeans very

10

seriously. Much of the copper, lead, silver and zinc exported by Peru is mined by Indians at those levels.

Down towards 3,000 metres (9,840 feet), climate and conditions grow gentler. The nights are often cold and sometimes frosty. But the days are fairly warm throughout the year. There is no real winter or summer; just a dry season and a wet season which remind visitors that they are in the tropics—though, of course, they are too high in the mountains to feel any tropical heat. Here, farmers can raise cattle and horses as well as the wool-bearing animals, and grow grain, vegetables and fruit of

Llamas tethered on the Peruvian Altiplano. Few crops can grow here, so the people raise animals—sheep, llamas and alpacas—for their wool and for meat

Quechua Indians threshing wheat. Towards 3,000 metres (10,000 feet), the climate makes it possible to grow fruit and cereal crops

the kinds that thrive in the cooler parts of Europe and other continents. The trees of cool temperate regions also grow well at these levels of the Andes, and several species have been imported, including poplars and willows from Europe, and eucalyptus (gum-trees) of types native to the cooler parts of Australia. The native trees here are mainly conifers, though these are low-growing, and look more like twisted shrubs than the tall, upstanding pines of conifer forests in northern Europe and North America.

Visitors hoping for tropical conditions must look much lower,

12

in the very deep valleys between some of the peaks, and in the very deep canyons that cut across some of the high plains. Irrigated with water from the rivers that shaped them, the floors of these valleys and canyons grow tropical and sub-tropical crops in temperatures twice as high as those of the slopes and basins 1,000 metres (3,280 feet) and more above them. Palm trees and fields of sugar-cane are a common sight.

The many rivers which rise in the Sierra are fed by melted snow from the peaks and ridges. They flow westward down to the Costa region or eastward down to the lower levels of the Montaña. The rivers flowing eastward are also fed by the rains of wet seasons which are really wet. On the eastern slopes of the Andes, more than 6,000 millimetres (240 inches) of rain can fall in a wet season of less than six months.

On the western slopes, over the Costa region, conditions are very different. There, even the wet seasons are fairly dry. So maps which show fifty-two rivers flowing from the mountains through the coastlands to the Pacific Ocean must not be taken very seriously. Forty-two of them have no water for most of the year, and as the Costa has practically no rain in most years it is very largely desert.

However, the Costa is not a hot desert. Although it lies wholly within the tropics, and mainly at low levels, day temperatures in most parts are usually between about 15 degrees and 20 degrees Centigrade (59 degrees and 72 degrees Fahrenheit) throughout the year. This is because the shores of Peru are kept cool by a cold ocean current which flows from Antarctica northwards towards the Equator. The current is named the Humboldt, after the German explorer who first charted it, but it is also called the Peruvian current, because it has so much influence on the climate of western Peru.

The influence is not limited to keeping the Costa fairly cool. It also keeps the region almost rainless. Moisture does rise from the current to form clouds, but these hardly ever break as rain. Instead they hang low over the desert, making the air very humid, and sometimes come down to earth as a thick mist called

A typical Andean valley, with massive mountain peaks towering high above

A view of part of the coastal desert region in the west of Peru

garúa. In some places, *garúa* moistens the desert soil enough to grow pasture for farm animals.

Towards the end of the year, the Costa's short northern shore is also touched by a warm ocean current which has the name *El Niño*. The words *el niño* (pronounced *el neen-yo*) mean "the baby", but if they are spelt with a capital *E* and a capital *N* they mean the Baby Jesus. That may seem a rather strange and unsuitable name for an ocean current. But it is understandable when we remember that most Peruvians are strongly religious people, and that the El Niño current usually reaches Peru at Christmas time.

As Peru is in the Southern Hemisphere, Christmas comes in the warmer half of the year. This is also the season when rain is most likely to fall. When the warm El Niño current meets

15

the cold Humboldt current, rain falls very heavily indeed. Usually, it falls only on and around the north-eastern corner of the Costa, where the town of Tumbes stands among coconut palms on a very fertile oasis. But in some years El Niño flows strongly enough to halt the Humboldt current and push it back, and then there is brief but disastrous flooding over the whole northern shore of the Costa. Crops on the many oases are destroyed. So too is wildlife. Fish which thrive in the cold current dislike the warmth of El Niño, and move away. And very great damage is done to the towns, which include Lima, Peru's capital city, and Callao, its main seaport.

Lima and Callao have over five million people between them, and the whole Costa region has about eight and a half million. Unlike the people of the Sierra, who are mostly full-blooded Indians and live by farming, most of these Costa people are town-workers descended from Spaniards or other Europeans, or from marriages between Europeans and Indians. As in most other South American countries, the people who are partly European and partly Indian are called *mestizos,* which means "mixed ones".

The Costa region also has Chinese and Japanese communities, and some people who are partly black. These partly black Peruvians are descended from marriages between black Africans and Europeans or Indians. The Africans were brought to Peru in earlier times to work as slaves on some of the big farming estates—but, of course, there are no slaves of any colour in Peru today.

16

Though most of the Costa people are town-workers, there is still a good deal of farming and fishing. Indeed, fishing is one of Peru's most important industries, and all the sea-fish are caught off the shores of the Costa. Another of the Costa's main industries is guano-digging. Guano is the hardened droppings of the millions of sea-birds who nest on Peru's offshore islands and feed on the fish of the Humboldt current. It makes an excellent fertilizer, and is still much used by farmers, even in the face of competition from modern artificial fertilizers.

The farms of the Costa are on about forty very fertile oases scattered about the region. On average, each oasis is about 150 square kilometres (58 square miles) in area, and is shared between big plantations growing mainly sugar-cane and cotton, and small general farms. In an almost rainless area of this kind, irrigation is essential. It comes mainly from the few rivers which

A typical small oasis town in the coastal desert

An irrigation scheme near Arequipa. Irrigation is essential in an almost rainless area of this kind

have a permanent flow of water. But two parts of the region get their water from further afield. These are in the north, near the Talara oilfields, and in the south near the iron-mining centres of Marcona and Acari. Farms in those areas are also irrigated by river water, but the water comes from rivers in the Montaña region on the other side of the Andes mountains. It is brought through the mountains by tunnels and canals, and fed into some of the dry river-beds of the Costa.

The Montaña region can easily spare the water, and could spare much more. With its many rivers fed by the melting snows and the rainfall of the eastern Andes, it is one of the wettest areas on earth. It is also one of the least known and least developed parts of South America, and certainly the most thinly-peopled region of Peru. With more than three-fifths of the country's land area, it has less than one in twenty of the country's people.

Many of that one-twentieth are primitive tribal Indians, who are a very different people from the settled, farming Indians of the Sierra region. Partly nomadic, they live in temporary huts along the many rivers, and get their food mainly by hunting, fishing and gathering the crops of jungle plants and trees. Some grow a few crops of their own, but most of the real farming in the Montaña is done by people who have moved in from other regions or from other countries. So too is most of the other work that is done in the Montaña—forestry, prospecting for minerals, and working the large oil deposits that have been found in recent years.

For visitors, perhaps the most interesting feature of the Montaña is its wildlife, especially if they have come there after visiting the Costa and the Sierra. In the Costa, there is little noticeable wildlife apart from armadillos with their bony "armour-plating", and a great variety of sea-birds. Nor does the Sierra have much wildlife except huge condor vultures in the sky and, on land, guanacos and vicuñas, which are both cousins of the more domesticated llamas and alpacas. However, the jungles and forests of the Montaña are the home of as wide a variety of insects, birds and animals as a visitor could wish to find—bright butterflies, monster beetles, chattering monkeys,

19

multi-coloured macaws and other parrots, snakes up to twelve metres (forty feet) long, peccaries, jaguars, tapirs, crocodiles and many more.

Sometimes, the Montaña region is called Amazonia. That is not an official name, but there is a very good reason for it. In the north, near lquitos—the region's one city—several of the rivers running down from the Andes join to form one great river which flows eastward out of Peru and into Brazil. Once in Brazil, it becomes even bigger—in fact, the widest river in the world, and the second longest. It is the famous Amazon, which from its sources in Peru crosses the whole northern width of South America, carrying water from the Andes on a 6,300-kilometre (3,900-mile) journey to the Atlantic Ocean. So it is possible to reach Peru on the west side of South America by sailing into the mouth of the Amazon on the east side, and small ships often make the journey. But that is not how the first Europeans reached Peru. Nor, as far as we know, did any of the country's earlier inhabitants come that way. Shall we take a backward glance at those early Peruvians?

Before the Spaniards

When Christopher Columbus sailed westward across the Atlantic Ocean and came to some of the islands between North and South America, he thought that the nearest continent was Asia, and that the islands lay off the coast of India. That is why the islands have been called the West Indies since about 1500, and why Europeans gave the name Indians to the native people of both American continents.

As it has happened, the name was less of a mistake than many of us have thought. It is not very likely that the first American "Indians" came from the country that is now called India, but it does seem certain that they were living in some other part of Asia before they crossed to North America about 25,000 years ago. They did not have to travel by sea. A wide strip of low-lying land then filled the gap between the north-east corner of Asia and the north-west corner of North America, so the migrants would have walked from one continent to the other.

These migrants were people of the Old Stone Age, nomadic and very primitive hunting and fishing families. Doubtless, many others followed them before the "land bridge" was deeply flooded by the waters now shown on maps as the Bering Strait, and some people believe that after the flooding there was no more migration from ancient Asia to the Americas. They say that the "land bridge" nomads were the ancestors of everybody living in the Americas before Europeans arrived.

However, it seems much more likely that some of the native Americans met by the early European settlers were not related to the "land bridge" migrants, but descended from quite different kinds of people who crossed the Pacific Ocean at different times during the thousands of years after the "land bridge" was flooded, and may possibly have landed at different points on the very long coastline of the two American continents. Otherwise, it is not easy to understand the great variety of physical and racial types, of languages, cultures and degrees of civilization which the early European settlers found among the many tribes and nations of American Indians. There were several hundred different languages, physical types ranging from the squat, slant-eyed Eskimos to the very tall and large-boned people who lived near the southern end of South America, and degrees of civilization that varied from primitive villages of headhunters and cannibals to cities in some ways as advanced as many in Europe.

Among the most advanced Indian communities was the Inca kingdom in Peru, centred on the magnificent city of Cuzco 3,500 metres (11,500 feet) up in the Sierra region. Quechua, the second official language of modern Peru, was the language of the Inca kingdom. In it, the word *cuzco* means navel, and the city was given that name because it was thought to be the central point of the Inca kingdom and empire, just as the navel is the central point of the human body.

22

The ruins of Sacsayhuaman, an Inca fortress near Cuzco

In 1532, at the time when the first Europeans reached Cuzco, it was a fairly new city—or rather it was an old city fairly recently and very grandly rebuilt. Nor was the Inca empire itself much older than the rebuilt city. Hardly a hundred years before Columbus crossed the Atlantic, the Inca kingdom was only one of many small kingdoms spread through Peru and the rest of north-western South America.

These kingdoms were communities of industrious farmers and very skilful craftsmen whose rulers were often tyrants living in great luxury. In some ways, such communities were not unlike the early city-states of ancient Greece. In other ways, they were surprisingly backward by comparison with the ancient Greek states. For example, though all the kingdoms of Peru depended on farming, and some gave great attention to improving their

23

crops, none of them knew about the plough. Their farmers worked the land with sharpened hardwood sticks, which were much slower and much less efficient than ploughs. The only other everyday farm tool seems to have been the hoe, with a bronze or a stone blade. There were—and still are—large deposits of iron in Peru, but until the Europeans arrived nobody knew how to work it, or how to make steel. Nor were wheeled vehicles used in pre-European times. The Indians had never thought of the wheel.

For many years, each of the small kingdoms was an independent country managing its own affairs, but as time went on two became richer and stronger than the others, and began to take control of them. The people of these stronger kingdoms were the Chimú (whose capital was the huge and wealthy coastal city of Chan-Chan) and the Quechua, whose capital city was Cuzco. The Quechua people are sometimes called the Incas, but that was never their real name. The Incas were the Quechua royal family, and the ruling king of the Quechua was always called the Inca. Nobody knows where the first Inca came from. The Incas themselves sometimes said that he rose from the water of Lake Titicaca. Whatever the truth behind that story (and several others) may be, we can feel fairly sure that the Incas began to rule the Quechua people around the end of the eleventh century A.D. In Europe, that was the century in which King William the Conqueror took the throne of England, and Christian Crusaders first set out for the Holy Land.

To the Quechua people, the ruling Inca was also a god. They

24

A view of Lake Titicaca. This lake holds a very important place in Inca folklore and mythology—the very first Inca was said to have risen from the waters of the lake

worshipped the sun, believing it to be the god Inti, and also believing that the Incas were Inti's family. Therefore, the ruling Inca—known as the Sapa Inca— was the earthly representative of his father Inti, and had complete power over everything and everybody. There was no room for democracy, or even for gentle opposition. The Inca kingdom was what we would now call a totalitarian state—perhaps the most completely totalitarian state that the world has ever seen.

The Inca kingdom was very successful in conquering its neighbours. So was its rival Chimú. They had swallowed up all the smaller kingdoms by about 1450, and Peru found itself divided between the two empires. However, even that did not

25

Part of the decorated mud wall of a temple near Chan-Chan, the capital of the Chimú empire

satisfy the Incas and the Chimú rulers. Each now wanted to swallow the other. The Incas, however, were clever enough to see that the Chimú people had one great weakness. As most of their territory was the coastal desert region, their food came mainly from oases watered by a well-planned and carefully-controlled irrigation system. So, instead of attacking cities as the Chimú expected, the Inca's army quietly captured and blocked all of the Chimú empire's key sources of precious irrigation water.

Faced with the prospect of drought-stricken oases and a very hungry year or more, the Chimú people lost interest in their leader's wish to rule the Inca's territories. After very little fighting the Chimú empire collapsed, and was overrun by the

Inca's army. The Inca empire now extended across the whole of north-western South America.

As the small kingdoms of Peru were in some ways like the city-states of ancient Greece, so did the Inca empire have something in common with the empire of ancient Rome. Both were famous for their buildings and their roads. Like Roman roads, the Inca roads ran straight. Indeed, they were often straighter than Roman roads. Because the wheel was unknown in the Inca empire, there was no need for roadmakers to change the line of the road so that it would not be too steep for wheeled traffic. Instead, they went straight on, cutting steps when they came to a slope that seemed too steep for people and animals to climb easily.

Part of a road built by the Incas in the desert. Like the Romans, the Incas were famous for their buildings and their roads

However, the roadmakers were not thinking of the comfort of people and animals when they decided that steps were needed. They were thinking of speed. The Incas wanted messages, goods, news, inspectors, spies and soldiers to travel the 5,200-kilometre (3,200-mile) length of their empire without delays. To reduce delays on steep hills, they had steps cut. For the same reason, they had cleverly designed suspension bridges built across steep-sided gorges and fast-flowing rivers.

The people who cut the steps and built the bridges and made the roads received no pay. Nor did anyone else in totalitarian Tahuantinsuyo—as the Incas called their empire. If people did the work they were told to do, and did it well, the state gave them food, clothing and shelter, and looked after them when they were too old to work. If they did not work well, or did not do what the state expected of them, they probably did not live to old age.

Everybody in the empire had to speak the Quechua language, whatever his native language might have been. Everybody had to worship the Sapa Inca as a god, and also the Inca's god Inti. If one of the Sapa Inca's officials decided that a family or even a whole community should move to another part of the empire they had to go, no matter how much they would rather have stayed where they were. On the other hand, nobody could change his living-place or his work of his own free will—unless he could show that he was an exceptionally able person. Then he would have a chance to become one of the high officials who controlled the day-to-day affairs of the empire, and saw that

28

the Sapa Inca's wishes were carried out. And then he would be allowed to wear the special gold ear ornaments which showed that he was a member of the ruling class.

For an official entitled to the ear ornaments, there were also other rewards and privileges, but money was not one of them. Like the wheel and the plough, money was unknown in the Inca empire. Huge quantities of gold and silver were mined in the Inca territories, but these metals were all used to make personal and household ornaments for the ruling class, and to decorate temples, palaces and other important buildings. Money could serve no purpose in a country where the government owned everything, and gave the people what it thought they needed— provided that they lived and worked exactly as the government ordered.

When the Incas had only a tiny kingdom around Cuzco, it was fairly easy to make the people accept their totalitarian system of government. But there were problems when the Inca kingdom became the Inca empire. In the conquered kingdoms, some of the people were more rebellious than the Quechua. They did not want the government to do all their thinking for them, to tell them what language they should speak, what work they should do, or how and when they should do it. And the further they were from Cuzco, the more difficult they were to control.

In the early 1500s, these problems grew until the ruling Inca, Huayna Capac, decided that the empire had become too big for one ruler to manage. Huayna Capac was then very ill and near the end of his life. Before he died, he divided the empire

29

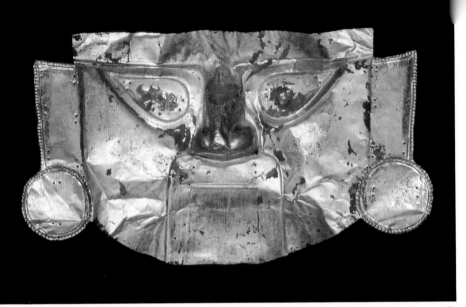

A funeral mask—an example of the beautiful gold ornaments made by the Incas

between two of his sons, naming one the ruling Inca of the north, and the other the ruling Inca of the south.

This division solved none of the problems. Each of the brothers soon made it clear that he wanted the whole empire for himself, and would fight to get it. So there was war between the north, under the Inca Atahualpa, and the south under the Inca Huascar. Atahualpa's army proved the stronger of the two. But before Atahualpa could enjoy any feeling of success and security a new menace to the whole empire arrived from outside its boundaries.

Conquerors and Colonists

A strange tale had been told by Quechua story-tellers for many centuries. It was this: at some time in the distant past the people around Lake Titicaca had been ruled by a group of kindly, bearded men with white skins. Nobody knew where these bearded white men had come from, but they had so much knowledge, and could do such remarkable things, that the Quechua and other Indians thought of them as gods. Then the warlike and overbearing Incas arrived, with the claim that the sun-god Inti and his ''son'' the leading Inca were the real gods. As if to prove this, the Incas trapped the white men on an island in Lake Titicaca, and killed most of them. However, the others escaped from the island and disappeared, leaving the Indians with faith that the white ''gods'' would one day come back to them.

That was the story. In the years around 1530 it was still believed by many of the people throughout the Inca empire. So few were surprised—and some were delighted—when they heard that bearded white men had been seen not far outside the empire's northern boundaries. There was even more delight in 1532 when, from oasis to oasis and up through the mountains, the news spread that bearded white men had actually arrived in the empire. They had come by ships which anchored off

Peru's short northern shore, in a river-mouth harbour which is now called Puerto (Port) Pizarro.

The port is called Pizarro after Francisco Pizarro, the leader of the bearded white men who landed there in 1532. These men were certainly not gods returning to their ancient home, although it took the Indians a little time to find that out. They were quite ordinary Europeans—Spaniards—who had sailed south from the new Spanish colony of Panama, on the Isthmus of Panama which joins the two American continents.

Panama was one of several small settlements founded on the isthmus by people anxious to explore and use the new lands reported by the navigator Christopher Columbus after his voyages across the Atlantic Ocean. Columbus himself was an Italian, but he was working for the King of Spain and commanding Spanish ships, so it seems natural enough that the Spaniards were the first Europeans to consider exploiting parts of the Americas.

They went first through the Caribbean Sea to the eastern side of Central America. There, they established small coastal settlements from which they sent explorers out into the jungle-covered mountains to the west. It was one of these explorers, Vasco Nuñez de Balboa, who discovered that they had settled on an isthmus—a narrow neck of land—separating the Caribbean Sea to the east from the Pacific Ocean in the west. Balboa also discovered a pass which led fairly easily right through the mountains and across the isthmus. At the western end of this pass the Spaniards founded the city of Panama, from which

Francisco Pizarro and his men set out in small ships to find the Inca empire.

However, they did not think of it as the Inca empire, or even as Tahuantinsuyo—the Incas' own name for the lands that they had conquered. The Spaniards called the empire *El Dorado*, a name which in Spanish can mean "Golden Country". Apart from some Christian priests who had come to work among the Indians, most of Pizarro's people were not real settlers. They had crossed the Atlantic to look for gold, silver and other precious minerals—treasure which they could mine for themselves, or take from other people. The Indians on the isthmus had told them of the huge quantities of precious metals which the Incas used to decorate their buildings, their equipment and themselves. So they thought of the Inca territories as *El Dorado*, the Golden Country.

Pizarro had only 183 men—so few that he could hardly hope to frighten the people of the oases and valleys on the way from the coast into the mountains, much less the Inca armies. He expected a troublesome journey. However, he had not allowed for the Indians' very strong belief in the story of the bearded white-skinned "gods" who had ruled some of their long-dead forefathers. Many of them genuinely took the Spaniards to be the old gods come back at last. So Pizarro's expedition travelled the first 500 kilometres (310 miles) into the mountains not only unharmed, but also with a following of friendly Indians.

It was different when they came to Cajamarca (now an important dairy farming centre) in a broad green valley 2,750

33

A gold ceremonial knife encrusted with turquoise. The conquistadors seized vast quantities of precious minerals and ornaments from the Incas

metres (9,000 feet) above the coast. There, they met the Inca Atahualpa with some of his army, on the way back to the north after a battle against the army of his brother Huascar, the Inca of the south. Atahualpa was not at all friendly. But, before he could do the Spaniards any harm, they captured him by trickery. To ransom him, they demanded a room stacked high with gold and silver. The ransom was paid, but the Spaniards found excuses for keeping Atahualpa in prison, and later found excuses for killing him.

For a time, the killing of Atahualpa made the Spaniards very popular in the southern half of the Inca empire. The southerners thought that it was a fair punishment for Atahualpa bringing

34

his army against them. But they were soon to find that the Spaniards too were an enemy. Like the Spanish invaders in other parts of South and Central America, Pizarro's men became known as *conquistadores*—conquerors. And now, helped by large numbers of Indians who had disliked all the Incas and their way of governing, the *conquistadores* overran the south as well as the north. It took them just three years to turn the whole Inca empire into the Spanish colony of Peru, with the new city of Lima as its capital.

The Spaniards had possession of Cuzco, the Inca capital, and could have used it as their own. But Cuzco is high in the mountains, and the Spaniards depended on sea communication with the Panama settlements and with Spain itself. So they preferred to have their capital city in the coastal region. Lima

A Spanish-style courtyard in Lima— a reminder of the Spanish conquest in the sixteenth century

is not right on the coast, but it has a very good seaport at Callao, only 13 kilometres (8 miles) to the west.

Although Pizarro's men had conquered the Inca empire in only three years, European settlers took very much longer to feel secure in Spain's new colony. At first there was fighting very like gang warfare between rival groups of *conquistadores*. Then there were rebellions by settlers against officials sent out from Spain to govern the colony in the name of the Spanish king. And there were far more serious rebellions by the remaining Incas and the many Indians who still supported them.

Indian rebellions were put down ruthlessly; often with very great cruelty. However, it is fair to remember that the Incas and their supporters were also guilty of extremely cruel behaviour, and that many of the atrocities blamed on the Spaniards were in fact committed by their Indian allies. These allies were ancient enemies of the Incas and they now took every chance of revenge for wrongs done to their people in the past. That does not excuse the Spaniards, but it does remind us to be a little careful of accounts in which all the Indians are "goodies", and all the Spaniards "baddies".

Peru was troubled by Indian rebellions for nearly three hundred years. During that time its capital, Lima, was the centre of colonial government for the whole of Spanish America. The colonial government grew less and less popular with the colonists as the years went on. This was mainly because more and more of the colonists were *criollos*—people of pure Spanish blood but born in America—who were treated as "second-class citizens" by the colonial government officials, who were usually Spaniards born in Spain. As for *mestizos*—the people of partly Spanish and partly Indian blood—they were hardly thought of as citizens at all until their numbers grew so great that they had to be noticed. But whether a colonist was a *criollo* or a *mestizo*, Spain and its colonial government discriminated against him very severely.

If he wanted to become a government offical himself, he could do so only at a very low level, and never hope to improve his position very much. If he was a trader exporting colonial products, he was forced to sell them in Spain. If he was a trader importing goods, he was forced to buy them in Spain. Whatever his work, in or out of the government service, he was taxed both heavily and unfairly.

Naturally enough, most of the *criollos* and *mestizos* thought that they would be better off if they could govern themselves. And, after some of Britain's North American colonies won their independence, the Spanish colonies in South and Central America were encouraged to try breaking with Spain. One by one, the colonies governed from Lima began making demands for independence. And when the Lima government sent soldiers to restrain them they fought back. Only Peru itself held back, and that was understandable. As Peru was the senior colony and the centre of colonial government, it was very strongly protected by the Spanish army and navy, and the Peruvian *criollos* and *mestizos* knew what had been happening to Indian rebels for nearly three centuries.

However, the newly-independent countries close to Peru could not feel secure while Peru was held by Spain and likely to be used as a base for attacks and invasions. So the republics of Chile and Argentina decided that they would have to use their own forces to win independence for the Peruvians.

The assault began by sea, when ships of the Chilean navy, commanded by the Scottish Admiral Lord Cochrane, began patrolling the coast of Peru and capturing or damaging whatever Spanish ships they could find. Then with eight warships and sixteen troopships—several with British or United States officers—and with four thousand soldiers under the Argentinian General San Martin, Cochrane sailed north to besiege Lima. The siege was not a very long one. Lima finally surrendered after a series of ''commando''-style attacks planned by Admiral

A frieze depicting Simon Bolivar *(second from left)* **and the Argentinian General San Martin**

A monument to General Antonio Sucre, in Ayacucho

Cochrane and carried out by a fairly small number of General San Martin's soldiers.

That was enough to make the Peruvians declare their country to be an independent republic. However, Peru's large highland region is very difficult to take from determined defenders. So most of the Spanish troops and officials retreated there after Lima fell, leaving the new republic with only the coastal desert region. And General San Martin passed the work of removing them to another republican leader, Simon Bolivar—after whom the present republic of Bolivia was named.

With his friend General Antonio Sucre, Bolivar organized and trained an army for independent Peru. In 1824 he led this army up into the Andes. The army, which included a good many

39

British mercenary soldiers, fought and defeated the Spanish forces in two battles. The first, at a height of 4,250 metres (nearly 14,000 feet) was near the lakeside town of Junin, in what is now the country's main mining area. The second, about 800 metres (2,600 feet) lower but still at a great height, took place near the town of Ayacucho. (Ayacucho is famous today not only as the place where the independence of Peru was finally won, but also for its university, its thirty-seven churches, its traditional craftwares, its magnificent religious processions during the Easter period, and its folk dancing to music played on instruments made from the horns of cattle.)

These two battles cleared the Spaniards from the highlands and put the whole country under an independent republican government. Even then about two thousand Spanish soldiers would not give up. They took possession of Real Felipe (Royal Phillip), a star-shaped fortress built to protect Lima's seaport Callao from attacks by pirates. They held out there for more than a year. When at last they were forced to leave, Bolivar said of their commander, José Rodil: "How we would have praised him if he had been one of us."

When Rodil and his men left the country, the last of Spanish colonial rule left with them. The *criollos, mestizos* and Indians were alone, facing the world as a nation. But were they ready for it?

The Independent Republic

When a country which is accustomed to colonial government becomes independent, its people often find that governing themselves is not as easy as they had imagined it to be. Some of them even begin to feel that they have made a bad bargain—that they would have been better off if their country had remained a colony.

That was certainly so in Peru. Under Spanish officials, the *criollos* and *mestizos* may not have liked the way in which their country was managed, but at least it was well-managed. They may have felt themselves treated as ''second-class'' or even as ''third-class'' citizens, but at least they could go about their daily lives knowing what to expect of the government, and what the government expected of them. However, when the Spanish officials had gone nobody seemed to know how the country should be managed—apart from a number of men who wanted to manage it for their own personal profit. Nor could the people know what kind of government to expect from one month to another. This month's president might easily be overthrown before he had a chance to put his policies into practice.

That is, if he had any policies. The presidents at that time came mainly from bands of soldiers who had helped to drive the Spaniards out, and who now expected the country to keep

41

them. So a president held office for only as long as his band of soldiers remained stronger than the other bands. In one year, seven different men called themselves President of the Republic at the same time. In its first thirty-five years of independence the country had nearly as many presidents as the U.S.A. elected in its first hundred years. Over the same period the republic's constitution—the rules by which a country is governed—was changed nine times.

Very few of this vast number of presidents knew anything about governing a country. Nor did they have experience or qualifications that might have helped. In fact, when the mother of one was told that her son had become president she said: ''Well, that's the last thing I'd have expected. If I'd seen it coming when he was a boy, I'd have sent him to school for a while.''

With presidents of that kind, and very few qualified or experienced officials to manage the business of government, the republic was soon very much in trouble, both at home and outside its boundaries. Its rulers caused a military invasion by its neighbour Chile, and made some bad mistakes in dealings with other ex-colonies. They also allowed unscrupulous people to take land from Indian farmers, leaving them with no way of making a living. This caused some of the poverty which is still today a great problem in the highland region. They also did little to revive the country's most important mining areas, which had been badly neglected during the years of fighting between the Spanish army and the republican rebels. These mines had been Peru's main source of income in colonial times.

By the late 1840s, with no money to repay huge sums which the republican governments had borrowed, the country was nearly bankrupt. It was saved by a very unlikely natural product—the vast quantities of sea-bird droppings called guano. During many thousands of years these droppings had formed a thick, hard crust over the arid, rocky little islands which lay close offshore.

The Indians had fertilized their fields with guano long before the *conquistadores* came to Peru, but the Spanish colonial government had never thought of exporting it. Nor had the republican governments considered doing so until the results of some scientific research caused great international demand

One of the many rocky islands off the Peruvian coast which are covered in guano and provide a useful source of fertilizer material

for plant-foods rich in the natural salts called phosphates and nitrates. These are both strongly present in guano, and fertilizer firms in Britain and other countries were soon offering Peru very large sums of money for the right to dig out the guano and ship it away.

Peru now became a fairly prosperous country, but its rulers were not always wise or honest in using the guano profits, and they continued to make mistakes. They let the country be drawn into a long and wasteful sea-war with Spain. No sooner was that over than a much more serious quarrel began, this time with Chile.

Chile, too, had been making a great deal of money from fertilizer material. This material was not guano, but a mineral called caliche, from which nitrates can be extracted. The caliche deposits are mainly in Chile's northern desert region, and at that time the boundaries between northern Chile and its neighbours Peru and Bolivia were not very clear. Bolivia and Peru therefore began to claim that a large part of Chile's nitrate deposits were really theirs, and threatened to take them by force. The Chileans were not to be bullied. They stood up to their aggressive neighbours, and successfully fought a four-year war with them. Peru and Bolivia both lost large sections of their territory. Although Chile later returned part of the Peruvian territory, it still keeps the very useful seaport of Arica. This means that many of Peru's imports and exports have to pass through Chilean territory, as the far south of Peru has no other seaport suitable for large ships.

Cutting sugar-cane, one of Peru's most important crops

After this fertilizer war—often called the War of the Pacific—the governments of Peru began to improve. At the same time, and with much help from Britain, the U.S.A. and France, a great deal of money was spent on development, so that the country need not depend wholly on guano. The neglected mining areas were revived, and new ones were opened up. A variety of factory industries was started. Roads and railways were built. Telegraph and telephone systems were introduced. And the owners of the large farming estates began to think more of growing and processing crops for export. Some of them were already growing sugar. Now many more started sugar plantations, or began to grow huge crops of cotton, which could be exported raw, or spun and woven into cotton cloth in some of the new factories.

All of that, with much other development, certainly made Peru a more prosperous country. But it was still not a very democratic one. Nor did the prosperity reach the large number of extremely poor people—perhaps more than half the country's population—who lived in the highland region.

Governments were usually controlled by a fairly small number of people who owned the sugar and cotton plantations, the mines and the large industrial undertakings. Any government which seriously tried to increase democracy or improve social conditions was overthrown, often violently. However, a government which fell in 1968 did so for the opposite reason. It had come to power with the promise of more employment, more land for small farmers, better housing and general social improvement. In the eyes of some people—including many army officers— it was being too slow in keeping its promise. So the army dismissed it, and replaced it with a group of senior officers.

The officers were genuinely anxious to improve social conditions. They set about doing so but—unlike the previous government—they tried to make sweeping changes too quickly for many of the people. There were serious riots which led to the end of army government and then, in 1980, to democratic elections under a new constitution.

The new constitution makes voting compulsory, so the present elected government genuinely represents the majority of all Peruvians aged eighteen and over. The President and both houses of parliament (which is called Congress) are elected separately but on the same day, for a term of five years. Congress has a total of 240 members. Sixty of these sit in the upper house (the Senate) and 180 in the lower house (the Chamber of Deputies).

Though the progressive army officers' government was overthrown, many of the changes which it introduced have been continued and developed by the present elected government. For example, the fact that about one-quarter of the Peruvian people cannot read and write suggests that many of them have never been to school. However, most of those are people who were children before 1972. In that year a law was passed saying that all Peruvian children must attend school between the ages of seven and sixteen. They may go to private schools if their parents are willing to pay fees, but if they go to government schools education is free.

Indian children in a school in Amazonia. Since 1972, education has been compulsory for all Peruvian children between the ages of seven and sixteen

The 1972 Law of Education caused a new and rather unusual change in school times and timetables. Because compulsory education brought a large and sudden rise in the number of children attending school, very few schools were large enough to hold all their pupils at the same time. Schoolwork therefore became shiftwork, some children going to school during the morning, others during the afternoon, still others during the evening. The evening sessions were shorter than the other two, and so evening pupils had to stay at school for a whole year longer than the others, to make up for their shorter daily work period. Since 1972, many new schools have been built, and others have been enlarged. But there are still a good many schools which can cope with their enrolment numbers only by putting their pupils on to shiftwork.

For pupils who want to stay at school after they have turned sixteen, there are now special schools called Higher Schools of Professional Education. Most people who go to these and complete the two-year course go on to a university. There are fourteen universities in the capital city, Lima, and about twenty others spread throughout the country.

Several of the universities are run by the Roman Catholic Church. So too are many of the schools, and all religious teaching must be Roman Catholic even in schools which are not run by the church. This is because Roman Catholicism is the state religion, and is allowed special privileges by the Peruvian constitution. Anybody who may wish to follow a different religion is free to do so, but in fact ninety-nine

A Spanish-style Catholic church in the province of Cuzco. Roman Catholicism is the state religion of Peru.

Peruvian people in every hundred are Roman Catholics.

Visitors used to the Roman Catholic Church in their home countries may be rather surprised at some of the ceremonies, festivals and church decorations they see in Peru. When the *conquistadores* arrived, the priests who came with them felt that their main task was to convert the pagan Indians to Christianity. They did this very successfully. To make the converts feel more at home in their new religion, the Church allowed them to fit some of their pagan customs and stories into Christian beliefs and ceremonies. As a result, it is not unusual to see in a religious procession the statue of a Christian saint surrounded by brightly-

49

costumed dancers whirling wildly to the music of traditional Indian wind instruments and drums. Nor is it unusual to find that some Indians are not quite sure of the differences between the Christian Virgin Mary and an ancient tribal mother goddess called Pachamama, or to see in churches pictures in which people from Bible stories have Indian faces, and sometimes Indian clothes. For example, the Baby Jesus is often seen wearing a woollen cap of a kind usually worn by Indians of the highland region.

In colonial times, Christian clergy in Indian communities were not only religious leaders and teachers. The poorer people also looked to them for medical treatment. Some of Peru's medical services today are still provided by the Church. However, as in most modern countries, the health of the people

Women bringing their babies for attention at a rural medical post — one example of modern health care in Peru

is now mainly a matter for the government. Recent Peruvian governments have been taking this responsibility very seriously. The country now has about 350 hospitals and 13,000 doctors—more than twice as many of each as there were in 1970. There are also well-equipped health centres in all the main towns and, in the more remote areas, over one thousand medical stations to which people may come for treatment and advice. Some of these are poorly-equipped and not very comfortable, but they are much used and very popular, particularly among mothers with babies or young children.

Unlike Britain, the U.S.A. and other advanced industrial countries, Peru has a large number of poor people who are very poor indeed. Most of these live in the farming areas of the highland region. In recent years the number of poor people in the more prosperous coastal region has also been growing steadily. That is not because the coastal region has become so much less prosperous, but because many thousands of people from the highlands have moved down to the coast hoping for a share in the prosperity. Unfortunately few of them have found it. They have merely joined the thousands of other unemployed and partly employed who live in the overcrowded and insanitary shanty towns on the edges of Lima and other coastal towns. And more will certainly follow them, in spite of warnings that they will probably be less comfortable and no richer in a straw shanty on the coast than they are in a mud-brick hut in the mountains.

The government provides some social welfare benefits for needy people in the shanty towns—*barriadas* as these settlements

51

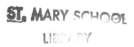

Barriadas, or shanties, in the old quarter of Lima. With thousands of people flocking to the cities in search of work, overcrowding and poor housing are almost inevitable

are usually called. Recently, it has also been trying to build proper and more healthy housing for them. But the shanties are still there and still overcrowded, and the people seem no less poor. Most cannot hope to become less poor while forty per cent of the country's working population cannot find a way to earn a living.

If they could find work, what would they do?

Earning a Living

In colonial times, the main work of Peruvians was farming and mining. More recently, fishing and manufacturing have also become important, but about half the Peruvian people still depend upon the country's farmlands for their living, while mineral exports provide nearly half of the country's earnings from overseas trade. So it can be said that the main work of Peruvians is still farming and mining.

However, Pizarro and his men would be disappointed at the amount of gold that is mined. There never was as much gold in Peru as they imagined, and very little is mined nowadays. On the other hand, they would be delighted at the output of silver. Peru heads the list of the world's silver-producing countries. It is also among the world's top ten producers of lead, zinc and copper.

The largest deposits of all those metals—and of several others—are around the town of Cerro de Pasco, on the bleak high plateau where the battle of Junín was fought. Here, the metals are not mined separately. They are all found in the same ore, and they are separated in smelting-plants at the other end of a railway line which crosses the plateau. Fuel for these plants comes from a coal-mine in the same area. This is said to be the highest coal-mine in the world.

Next to copper, silver, lead and zinc, the most important mineral deposits now being worked in Peru are of iron and oil. Until 1979, most of the country's oil (petroleum) came from the wells around the refinery and oil-port at Talara, on the north coast, and was hardly enough to meet the country's own needs. Since then, Talara has been linked by pipeline with newly-opened oilfields in the jungles of the Montaña region. Peru now earns nearly as much from exporting oil as it does from exporting copper, silver, lead and zinc.

Production of iron—Peru's other important mineral—is mainly a lowland industry, based on mines in the southern coastlands. Not very long ago, all the iron taken out of these mines was carried by road to two small nearby seaports, and then shipped direct to other countries. Now, much of it goes

Open-cast mining near the town of Cerro de Pasco. Large deposits of copper, lead, zinc and silver are found here

An oil-well near Talara, on the north coast. Until 1979, most of the oil produced in Peru came from this area

north to another Peruvian seaport, Chimbote. There, it is treated at a fairly new mill which supplies Peru and some export customers with a wide range of bars, girders, galvanized sheets and other iron and steel products.

The Chimbote mill uses locally-mined coal, and hydro-electricity from a power-station whose generators are driven by the water of the River Santa—one of the few coastland rivers that has a large and always reliable flow.

Since the first products left the mill in 1958, the population of Chimbote has risen sixty times, from 4,000 to 240,000, but the rise has not been wholly because of the mill. Over the same period, Peru moved to the top of the list of the world's fishing countries. And Chimbote became its main fishing-port, with factories producing most of the fishmeal which Peru exports in very great quantities. Countries which import fishmeal use it for feeding cattle and other animals. It is a very nourishing food, with a very powerful smell. The smell is particularly noticeable while the meal is being manufactured—and that explains why tourists and others who visit Chimbote rarely stay longer than they have to.

Other fishing-ports along the coast became prosperous at the same time as Chimbote did, so each of these ports now has its colony of highland people living in hastily-built *barriadas.* Some of the newcomers managed to find a share of the prosperity. But in 1982 the ocean current, El Niño, drove away most of the small herring called *anchoveta,* from which fishmeal is made. This was not the first time that Peru's fishing industry had suffered from El Niño, but it was by far the worst, especially as the industry had been taking too many fish from the sea in good years. In addition, the military government of the 1970s had made some mistakes in trying to run the industry as a government business. As a result, the fishing-fleet is now only half as big as it was, and Peru has dropped from first place to sixth on the list of fishing countries. That, of course, means that very few of the highland farming people who moved hopefully to the fishing-ports can now be any better off than they were.

The problems of the highland farming people began in colonial times. Then, as now, only about six per cent of the highland region was suitable for farming, and much of the six per cent was land of fairly poor quality. This poorer land was given to Indian communities who shared it among themselves

A fishing fleet off Chimbote, Peru's main fishing port

in small plots, each just big enough to feed an average family in a good season. The rest of the farmland was divided into very large estates called *haciendas* or *latifundios,* and given by the colonial government to Spanish colonists. Such extensive land-holdings needed great numbers of workers, and these were recruited from among Indians who had no land of their own, or too little to keep them in food.

An Indian worker of this kind was in much the same position as a serf in the old feudal systems of Europe. He usually had no wages, but worked for his food and shelter, and for the use of a small piece of land; and once he had joined an estate he could not move away without the owner's permission. In fact, he was not very different from a slave.

57

Some people thought that conditions would improve when Peru became an independent republic, but they were disappointed. Republican governments could not control estate-owners as firmly as the colonial officials had done, and conditions very soon grew worse instead of better. Many more Indians were now made landless and often workless by estate-owners who wanted more land and did not mind breaking the law to get it.

For many years there was much talk by politicians about redistributing the land—taking some from those who had too much, and giving it to those who had too little. But it was not until the 1960s that governments began any serious attempts to do so. Some of these attempts were not very popular and made little progress, but on the whole they have been fairly successful. Most of the big estates are now run as co-operatives. This means that the people who do the work now share the profits as well as receiving wages and keeping the small pieces of land which the estate-owners had previously given them instead of wages.

Those estate-owners who themselves are still farming are doing so on a much smaller scale. New land laws allow nobody to own more than 150 hectares (370 acres) in the very dry areas that need irrigation, and about 50 hectares (122 acres) in areas that are well-watered in normal seasons.

Of course, very few Peruvian farmers have as much land as that. Estate-workers and those who shared land in the Indian communities were lucky to have more than one hectare (2.4 acres), and the more prosperous small farmers who gave money or a share of the crops as rent for their land usually had about five hectares (12 acres). These farmers no longer pay rent for their land, because it is now their own. It was bought by the government and given to the farmers at about the same time as the big estates became co-operatives.

In these and other ways, nearly 7,000,000 hectares (17,000,000 acres) of land has been handed over to the people who work on it, but there are still a great many very poor people in rural Peru. Some of these have no land at all. Others can make only a very bare living from the land that they own or share, because its quality is very poor. Some of it is poor naturally. Much of the rest is poor because the estate-owners who once owned it had so much land that they could do very well for themselves without looking after it properly.

As a result, thousands of rural people still live almost wholly on soups and porridges made of maize (Indian corn) and less appetizing grains, dried beans and potato starch. Many eat meat only once or twice a year, at Christmas and other religious festivals—and the meat is usually guinea-pig.

These are the people who have been going down to the coast in large numbers to swell the *barriadas* around the big towns and the fishing-ports—especially during the long drought which has struck much of Peru in recent years. In addition, some have gone in the opposite direction, down the eastern side of the Andes to the Montaña region. Indeed, the government has been encouraging people to settle in the under-populated Montaña, because it has plenty of good land, natural foods (including

An Aymara Indian woman and her children, preparing their meal

bananas) which practically grow themselves, and opportunities for employment in development schemes.

However, people from the Sierra do not seem to find the Montaña very attractive—perhaps because the native Indians and much of the region itself both seem so far from civilization. They prefer going down to the coast, and taking the chance that they will be able to earn a living in the fishmeal factories, or in the capital city Lima and its seaport Callao. Here, where more and more skyscrapers throw dark shadows over beautiful old Spanish buildings, are to be found more than one-quarter of the Peruvian people, about three-quarters of the country's commercial activities, and nearly four-fifths of its factories.

60

Coast and Capital

With a population of nearly 4,800,000, Lima is the only city in Peru which can count its people in millions. No other Peruvian city has yet reached the half million mark. Of the ten cities whose people number between 100,000 and about 400,000, six are in La Costa, the coastal region. As Lima is also in La Costa, that gives the region a number of city-dwellers greatly out of proportion to its size. Although La Costa is less than half the size of the highland region, and would fit more than five times into the Montaña, it has nearly as many people as both, and most of those people live in cities and towns.

However, the population of a sea-trading country with a broad spine of high rugged mountains could hardly have developed in any other way. The conquistador Pizarro saw that in 1535, when he chose for the capital city a site near enough to the Pacific Ocean to make transport to and from ships easy, but far enough inland to make attacks from the sea difficult. The site is also sheltered from inland winds by a curve of bare hills, and watered by the Rimac, one of the coastal rivers which never stop flowing. Sometimes—especially when the ocean current El Niño is being troublesome—the Rimac's flow is violent and very high, and it spreads damaging floods over parts of the city and its surrounding oasis.

The name Rimac comes from one of the Indian languages. It means "the talker", and seems to have been given to the river because of the gentle chattering sounds of its waters when they are not in flood.

Though it hardly looks so in print, the name Rimac is also the present name (Lima) of the city which spreads out from both of its banks. Some American Indians—like many people in eastern Asia—find it hard to pronounce the sound of the letter *r*. When they try, the result is more like the sound of the letter *l*, so that the word Rimac sounded something like *Limac* to colonists who heard local Indians saying it. In time, the Europeans began using that pronunciation themselves, and then lazily dropped the final *c*, thus leaving their capital city with the name Lima.

However, Francisco Pizarro called his city neither Rimac nor Limac nor Lima. To him, it was *El Ciudad de los Reyes,* which means the "City of the Kings." People are sometimes puzzled over which kings Pizarro meant. Some say that he must have been thinking of the kings of Spain. Others wonder if they were the rulers of the small kingdoms that the Incas conquered to make their empire. In fact, they were neither. Pizarro founded his city on the day of the Christian religious festival called Epiphany. That is the day on which the Three Wise Men from the East brought gifts to the Baby Jesus. But, of course, the Three Wise Men are also known as the Three Kings—and those were the kings Pizarro had in mind.

The City of the Kings was planned in the style of towns in

The Church of La Merced (Mercy) in Lima. Lima was founded on Epiphany Day and because of this was originally called the City of the Kings

Spain, with straight streets running out from a main square, and crossing each other at right angles to make blocks which extend about 150 metres (490 feet) in each direction. As in most towns or cities by a river or the sea, the main square is close to the waterfront—although, rather strangely, the railway has been allowed to run between the square and the river bank. This means that the rear of the huge presidential palace, which fills one side of the square, overlooks the yard of the central railway station.

However, it also overlooks a very strong and handsome stone bridge, the oldest of four which cross the Rimac in central Lima.

The presidential palace in Lima, built on the site of Pizarro's own house

This bridge is called, quite simply, the Stone Bridge, but some people say that a better name would be the Egg Bridge. The builders mixed their mortar with over a million egg-whites, in the belief that this would help to bind the stone blocks together more firmly.

Among the skyscrapers and the many other developments of four hundred and fifty years, the plan of Pizarro's city is still clear. Most of the buildings which interest visitors are still within its one hundred and seventeen blocks. But, even here, nearly all the buildings themselves date from long after Pizarro's time. Some—including the president's palace built on the site of Pizarro's own house—belong to our own century.

Not all these changes are the result of modernizing and development. Lima, like the rest of Peru, is in an earthquake zone, and many of its older buildings have had to be restored or replaced because of earthquake damage. The colossal Roman Catholic cathedral (like the president's palace, it fills one whole side of the main square) has been among the chief victims. After taking more than one hundred years to build, it was badly damaged less than forty years later, and completely destroyed within another fifty years. Rather surprisingly, the tall twin towers of a church just a few minutes' walk from the cathedral stood firm through both those earthquakes and several more.

Called Santo Domingo (Saint Dominic's), this twin-towered church is part of a monastery which in Lima's early years was also the University of San Marcos, the first university in either of the American continents. Now moved to a large park in the newer half of the city, San Marcos has thirty thousand students, and is still growing.

Most people who visit Santo Domingo hardly remember that it was the birthplace of the first American university. They go there as pilgrims to the burial place of the Christian religion's first American saint—a Spanish woman born in Peru. She is now the country's patron saint, and is known as Saint Rose of Lima. Santo Domingo is also the burial place of the first *mestizo* American saint, a *mestizo* whose mother was a Peruvian Indian. Known as Saint Martin de Porres, he is now regarded as a patron saint of race relations.

So far, Peru's fairly large black community has not produced a saint, but it has produced a religious picture which—so many people believe—can work miracles. The original was painted by an ex-slave on a wall of the house where he lived as a member

65

The archbishop's palace in Lima. Note the Spanish influence in the architecture

of a black Christian brotherhood, and that wall was the only one left standing after several earthquakes had shaken the house. Since then, a protective church has been built round the wall. For three days of each October a huge gold-framed copy of the picture is carried through the streets of Lima by a team of thirty men dressed in purple robes. Thirty men are needed because the picture and the heavy silver platform on which it rests weigh over 900 kilograms (about 2,000 pounds).

Showered with flowers thrown from windows and balconies,

and followed by bands, singers and a great throng of admiring people, the picture is moved very slowly around the city, stopping for a few minutes at almost every street corner, and sometimes between corners. Most streets are full of spectators watching the picture pass, and of pedlars selling traditional festival foods of many kinds, but especially one called *turrón de Doña Pepa*—"Madame Pepa's nougat". In the evenings, the procession keeps moving until well after dark, with torchlight and candleflames making it look, from a distance, like a massing of glow-worms.

As Peru is in the southern hemisphere, October is the first month of spring. This makes it a time for many other activities and festivities besides the picture procession. For example, it sees the beginning of the season for surfing and many other water sports on the excellent beaches lying north and south of Lima's

The Flower Market in Lima

seaport Callao, and is also the first month of the main bull-fighting season. Unlike their Chilean neighbours, the Peruvians like to watch bull-fighting in the old Spanish style, a style which is certainly dangerous and, in the opinion of many people, very cruel. The main centre for the sport is a huge old bullring in Lima, on the north side of the Rimac. Here too there is a museum of bull-fighting, although there is also another of these among the very fine range of museums south of the river. Cock-fighting, now banned in many countries, is still legal in Peru, and for this too the main centre is in Lima.

In terms of Peru's progress and prosperity, perhaps the most important October activity is the International Pacific Fair, an exhibition of trade and industry held for two weeks on a 20-hectare (50-acre) fairground in the growing industrial area which spreads between Lima and Callao. Lima and Callao are linked by road and rail, the railway being one of the oldest in South America. However, there is now very little rail transport in the rest of the Costa region, as all the coastal towns are linked by the Peruvian section of the international motor road called the Pan-American Highway. This runs the whole length of the region on its way north and south through the two American continents, and is joined by east-west roads which link it with the Sierra and Montaña regions.

Though they vary a great deal in size, the Peruvian towns and cities along the Pan-American Highway are all much the same in their surroundings and activities. Each is on, or close to, an oasis. Each is mainly concerned with processing and marketing local produce—chiefly fish and fishmeal if it is a town on the sea; sugar, cotton, rice, tropical and Mediterranean fruits and general farm crops if it lies inland. Even paper-milling towns, such as the small seaport Paramonga, use a local product as their raw material. That is bagasse, the dried waste cane from sugar refineries.

There are exceptions, such as Chimbote with its iron and steel mill, Talara with its oil refinery, Trujillo with car assembly and engineering works. The main industries of these places and several others use raw materials brought from other areas or other countries. But, in general, the towns of Peru's desert region deal in the produce of their own oases and fishing-grounds—and that produce includes most of the food eaten by the region's 9,500,000 people. Among it are two common crops which, though small vegetables with small names, are very important to most Peruvians. They are *aji* and *ajo*—meaning

Part of the Pan-American Highway, along Peru's coast

chillies and garlic. On Peruvian menus there are very few soups, stews and savoury sauces that do not contain one or other of these, or more often both.

However, the taste for *aji* and *ajo* does not mean that Peruvians dislike sweet foods. Children in some other countries may be surprised to learn that rice pudding is very popular here; but more typically Peruvian is *mazamorra morada*, which is mainly purple sweet corn and dried fruits held together by sweet potato flour, and flavoured with cloves, cinammon and lemon.

In spite of much unemployment, La Costa is the most developed, progressive and modern of Peru's three natural regions. Because of this, visitors sometimes forget that the Indians of Peru began their history on the coast, and that the region holds a great deal that is very ancient—often more ancient, and sometimes more interesting, than the much better-known remains of the Inca empire in the highland region.

Among these coastal relics are the ruins of cities, temples and irrigation systems; thousands of pieces of very fine pottery, sculpture and stone-carving; wall-paintings, tools and weapons, and one of the world's great mysteries.

The mystery is in the desert surrounding a small oasis that contains the town of Nazca, towards the southern end of the region. It is a vast stretch of fairly level, stony ground which people at some time in the distant past have marked out with the shapes of birds, animals and geometrical figures. Some of the shapes are four kilometres (2.5 miles) or more in length—

The shape of a humming-bird marked out in the desert near the town of Nazca

so long that the subjects cannot be recognized by a person looking at them from ground level. They become clear only when they are seen from the air, and there are aeroplane services which allow visitors to do this.

Nobody knows who drew the Nazca shapes, or why. Nor, since they can be seen as a whole only from aircraft, is it certain how they could have been drawn so accurately many centuries before aircraft were invented. However, there is no doubt that the people who planned them must have known much of the practical mathematics needed by modern civil engineers. So perhaps the drawings are a sign that this region too had some of the white-skinned bearded ''gods'' whose great knowledge and remarkable achievements so astonished the ancient peoples of the highland region that rises directly to the east of Nazca.

The High Central Region

Until 1970, people travelling from the central coastlands to the highland region by train had the choice of two routes. They could choose a line which began at Lima, or a more northerly line which began at Chimbote. The line from Lima climbed through the valley of the River Rimac, while the line from Chimbote followed the valley of the River Santa, below the double summit of the extinct volcano Mount Huascarán, which is the highest peak in the Peruvian Andes.

Now, however, there is no choice of line. In 1970, an earthquake shook the slopes of Mount Huascarán and its neighbours, and sent a disastrous avalanche crashing and rolling down into the valley. This tremendous fall of ice, snow, rock and mud killed over twenty thousand people, buried two towns and several villages so deeply that only a small part of a church roof and the tops of three palm trees could still be seen, and damaged the railway so badly that the line has never been re-opened. That leaves only the line from Lima for those who want to climb the Andes from the central coastlands by train—and a wonderful line it is.

Called the Central Line, it was built for a British company by a United States engineer using workmen who were mainly Chinese, and who took twenty-three years to complete it at an average of eighteen kilometres (eleven miles) each year. That is a very slow rate for laying a railway, and people who take the daily train from Lima up to the terminus town of Huancavelica soon understand why the work was not done more quickly. In its length of 550 kilometres (340 miles), the workmen had to cut large numbers of zigzag ledges on the mountainsides, and also to dig sixty-six tunnels and build sixty bridges—many of these at heights where most people begin to suffer from the mountain sickness called *soroche*.

The highest station on the line, at 4,781 metres (15,675 feet), is also the highest standard gauge railway station in the world. It stands at one end of the highest tunnel on the line, which is one metre (3.3 feet) higher than the station, while the line itself reaches a height of 4,818 metres (15,806 feet). However, the road which follows roughly the same route as the railway climbs higher still. At the Anticona Pass it reaches 4,843 metres (15,879 feet)—which means that travellers using the pass are well above the height of Mont Blanc in the French Alps (the tallest peak in western Europe).

The highest tunnel goes through the flank of a mountain which since 1893 has been called Mount Meiggs. It was given that name in honour of Henry Meiggs, the great United States railway engineer who planned and built the line. On the summit of this mountain, travellers have the rather strange sight of a flag that keeps perfectly still, however strongly the winds blow. It is the flag of Peru—a vertical white stripe between two red stripes, with the Peruvian coat-of-arms in the centre of the white

This sign marks the highest point reached by any railway in the world

stripe—and it keeps perfectly still because it is made not of cloth, but of strong sheet metal. Cloth would not withstand for long the fierce weather conditions at these levels of the Andes.

The terminus of the line, Huancavelica, is an old colonial mining town whose mercury-mines are no longer of any importance. Neither the town nor the surrounding district has much to interest visitors, so very few travellers go to the end of the line. Instead, they leave the train at Huancayo, one of the three highland towns with more than 150,000 people. Huancayo is the marketing centre for a large and fertile valley which has a Mediterranean climate (dry warm summers followed by rainy winters), and grows nearly half of Peru's total wheat crop. The valley is also the site of a new hydro-electricity works,

74

and a grazing-ground for large numbers of alpacas and llamas. The wool of these animals is spun, dyed and woven at factories in Huancayo, and also by country people in their own homes, using traditional hand-operated equipment.

Visitors usually find that the main attraction of Huancayo is its Sunday market, at which Indians from farms in the valley try to sell brightly-coloured woollen blankets and clothing, handcraft products, and many kinds of fruit, vegetable and grain.

Among the handcraft products, Huancayo's speciality is the *maté*, a carved and painted gourd. These are offered in many shapes and sizes and for a wide range of uses, with all kinds of decoration from simple line patterns to delicate and intricate pictures. For example, your *maté* may be a drinking-cup, a soup-bowl, a honey-pot, a kitchen storage-jar, or just a piece of house decoration. In other parts of South America, but especially in Argentina and Brazil, *matés* are used mainly as a cup from which liquid is sucked through a tube—and that is why a very popular South American drink (rather like a herbal tea) is called *yerba* (or *hierba*) *maté*. The name means "herb for gourds".

North of Huancayo, towards the bird-haunted Lake Junin and on a branch line of the Central Railway, is the smoky and rather grimy town of La Oroya. La Oroya is one of the very few industrial towns in the highland region. It has the smelting-works which extracts silver, lead and other metals from ores mined in the Cerro de Pasco area, on the far side of the bleak and damp high grasslands that surround Lake Junin.

The smelting works in the town of La Oroya. Silver, lead and other metals are extracted from ores mined in the area of Cerro de Pasco

Southward from Huancayo, the country becomes as dry as the plain around Lake Junin is damp. Here, about 300 kilometres (190 miles) from Huancayo down a narrow and winding road that is often blocked by landslides, is a handsome yellowstone town built in the old Spanish style. This is Ayacucho, where the republican colonials and the soldiers of the Spanish king fought their last battle before Peru became a republic. Every year the anniversary of the republican victory is celebrated on the battlefield, with local schoolchildren and soldiers re-enacting the battle.

Like Huancayo, Ayacucho specializes in carving and painting

76

matés, but its many craftsmen also make leather goods, human and animal figures in locally-quarried marble, and filigree silverware. All of these, and many other things too, are on sale at the town's popular Sunday market.

Sunday markets are a feature of town life throughout the highlands. Indeed, without them many more of the region's Indians would be below the poverty line. As in Huancayo and Ayacucho, most markets are known for one or two local specialities. Whatever these specialities may be, customers can feel sure that they will also find vendors with large stocks of blankets, ponchos and hats. The hats are often in shapes and styles usually thought to be for men—trilbies of felt or straw, for instance, and several variations on the bowler or derby. But,

Bread and colourful hand-woven blankets on sale in a Sunday Market

in fact, most of these are bought and worn by Indian women. Women say that they prefer them because they are more protective to the hair and the head in the cold and windy highland climate, but there are not many who deny that people also find them very becoming.

We have visited Ayacucho earlier, and so can leave it now for a glance at Cuzco on our way to Lake Titicaca. For those who are interested in the Incas and their civilization, Cuzco and the towns around it are—as they were for the Incas themselves—the heart of Peru. Mainly because of earthquakes, none of Cuzco's Inca buildings remains exactly as it was; most have been reduced to their foundations, with perhaps a wall standing here and there. However, the most recent serious earthquake,

A general view of the town of Cuzco, which was once an important Inca settlement

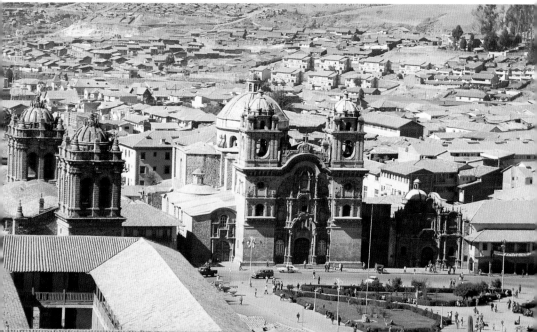

The famous Inca Temple of the Sun in Cuzco. A Christian church was built over the top of the temple, and the combination of Spanish and Inca styles can be seen clearly here

in 1950, had the opposite effect. It damaged a very large church which stood on the site of the famous Inca Temple of the Sun, and the damage revealed that much of the temple was still standing. Its walls had merely been plastered over, and decorated for use as the walls of a church.

Since then, the church authorities have allowed archaeologists to excavate, and they have uncovered a great deal more of the old temple. These remains are now on view to visitors. With walls and foundations to be seen in other parts of the city, they show what truly remarkable builders the Incas were.

From Cuzco, a straight journey south by road or rail leads to the huge Lake Titicaca and the lakeside town of Puno—an old colonial mining town which was once known for the "wild west" behaviour of its people. Its modern inhabitants, who are

79

much more peaceable, number about 45,000. They are known for their market, which has a very wide range of woollen products, for the *sicu,* a musical instrument made of reeds from the lake, and for their festivals, some of which are not connected with the Christian church. One of these is a dancing festival in which people are dressed and masked as devils; in another they go back to Inca times, and act out the story of the first Inca who rose from the water of the lake.

Some of Puno's inhabitants, a small tribe of Indians called Urus, live not in the town but on floating islands, or what appear to be floating islands. In fact, these "islands" are very large rafts made from reeds which grow in the lake. The Urus also make boats from these reeds. The Norwegian anthropologist Thor Heyerdahl came here to study Uru boats before he built an ocean-going reed vessel for a recent voyage in the Arabian

The floating "islands" — large rafts made of reeds — on which the Uru Indians of Lake Titicaca live

Two Uru Indian children making a reed boat on the shores of Lake Titicaca

Sea. Heyerdahl's famous ocean-going raft *Kon Tiki* was even more Peruvian. It was made on the coast at Callao, with huge logs of balsa wood cut from the great trees of the Montaña forests.

West of Lake Titicaca, at the foot of the very beautiful volcano El Misti, and flanked by two others, spread the low white buildings of Arequipa, the second largest city in Peru. The three volcanoes are all over 5,600 metres (18,300 feet) high, but Arequipa itself is in a deep and fertile valley only about 2,380 metres (7,800 feet) above sea-level. That gives it a warmer and much more reliable climate than other highland cities, with very little rainfall. The valley uses an irrigation system to keep its

81

A view of Arequipa, at the foot of the volcano El Misti

grain crops and Mediterranean fruits growing, and to water its herds of dairy cattle and its groves of Australian gum trees.

Arequipa was founded by the Incas, but earthquakes have left very few remains of the famous Inca stonework. Most of the buildings are in the Spanish style, and stand very low—most no more than one storey high. That is to lessen the likelihood of damage from earthquakes, which happen often in this part of Peru. The building material is mainly a lightweight stone, very white in colour, which is quarried from the lava of the volcanoes. For this reason, Arequipa has a second name—the White City.

Arequipa, an important staging-post when most goods

travelling between the highlands and the coast were carried by mules and llamas, has since become the "capital" of southern Peru, and is now mainly a manufacturing and commercial city, with factories producing canned milk and other processed foods, woollen and nylon cloth, plastics, steel, chemicals, cement, radios and bicycles.

Factory wages have attracted many people from the fairly poor towns and villages around Lake Titicaca. These people—often still unemployed—live in *barriadas* on the fringes of the city. With other newcomers, they have caused Arequipa's population (about 450,000) to increase eight times since the Second World War.

From Arequipa, the railway line runs down to the Pacific Ocean, linking the highlands with the oases, mining communities and small seaports of the southern coastlands. In the opposite direction it climbs back to Lake Titicaca, and then along the upper eastern slopes of the Andes to the most impressive and complete of all Inca ruins—the city of Machu Picchu.

Machu Picchu straddles a grassy ridge about half-way up a peak called Huayna Picchu, with irrigated terraced fields dropping steeply to valleys as much as 430 metres (1,400 feet) deep. The city was a staging-post on the Inca road from Cuzco down to what is now called the Montaña region. From time to time people have put forward various other reasons for its existence—some of them very strange reasons—but all that has been established is that it was a staging-post, and perhaps (towards the end of its life) a place of refuge for some of the last Inca supporters to defy the Spaniards.

Now, it is merely the highlight of a holiday in Peru for the thousands of tourists who want to see what an Inca city looked like, without any later additions or overbuilding. Nothing is covered up. And all of the buildings are complete, apart from the upper stones of walls and the thatched roofs—which are easy enough to imagine.

Such a large part of the city is still standing because this eastern side of the Andes is so different from the desert western side. The rainfall here is regular and heavy. The rivers are never

A view of the Inca city of Machu Picchu

dry, and often in flood. So immediately below the tree-line (the level at which temperatures are warm enough for trees to grow), trees really do grow. At around 3,000 metres (9,800 feet), below a belt of almost continuous fog, thick forest and undergrowth begin to cover the mountainsides. This zone, known as *La Ceja de Montaña* (the Montaña's Eyebrow) is the divide between La Sierra (the highland region) and La Montaña (the woodland region), and Machu Picchu lies within it.

Therefore, when the last of the Incas' supporters left the city, the jungle was quick to move in. After a very few years Machu Picchu was so overgrown that it became a lost city, and it remained a lost city until 1911, when a United States explorer found it almost by accident.

Since then, more Inca remains have been uncovered, and it seems very likely that others will be found as more of the Montaña's forests and jungles are cleared to keep a large timber market supplied, and to open up land for farming.

Under the "Eyebrow"

Nobody knows exactly when the Incas began to take an interest in the Montaña. Nor do we know all the reasons why they built roads with comfortable staging-points down the densely-wooded eastern Andes to the even more densely-wooded tropical lowlands around the upper streams of the River Amazon. But we do know some of the reasons. Like the Spaniards who replaced them, the Incas wanted silver and gold and there were certainly silver and gold deposits in the Montaña. There still are—and deposits of less valuable but very useful metals, too. The Incas also liked to decorate themselves with large brightly-coloured feathers, and the Montaña has the largest brightly-feathered birds in the world. But far more important than the feathers were products from some of the jungle vegetation. These included ingredients for medicines and ointments, colouring matter for dyes and paints, and fruits which could not be grown in the cool highlands.

There was also *coca*—not to be confused with cocoa, another product of the Montaña, or with the soft drink Coca-Cola. *Coca* is the Quechua Indian name for a bush of the flax family, which grows wild in parts of the Montaña. We know now that the leaves of the *coca* bush can be treated to produce a drug that is very dangerous, but the Indians did not know that. What

86

A modern actor dressed as the Sapa Inca. As can be seen here, the Incas used large, brightly-coloured feathers from birds in the Montaña region in their costumes

they did know was that if they dried *coca* leaves and then chewed them when they were tired or hungry, they stopped being tired or hungry. That made *coca* leaves seem almost a necessity to people who were sometimes overworked and underfed by both Indian and Spanish masters; and the leaves are still chewed by many of Peru's very poor people. However, *coca*-sellers no longer rely on gathering leaves from wild plants. *Coca* has become a farm crop, and a herbal tea made from the leaves is said to be a remedy for mountain sickness.

Missionaries began work among the very primitive Indians

87

of the Montaña almost as soon as the Spanish *conquistadors* had taken Peru, but few Europeans followed them. It was not until the nineteenth century that Europeans began to take any real interest. The first groups who came were looking for two other natural products of the forests—the sap of one tree and the bark of another. The sap was the milky and sticky latex from the rubber tree, which hardens into rubber. The bark, from a tree called cinchona, was used to make quinine, the medicine which helps to cure malaria and other fevers.

Both latex and cinchona bark may still be gathered from wild trees in the Montaña forests, and both are also obtained from cultivated trees. However, neither is as much in demand as it used to be. So the Montaña's main town, the city of Iquitos, might now be a depressed area if two American visitors—Robert Ford and David Fyfe—had not become interested in a dome-shaped hill called Aguas Calientes.

Aguas Calientes is the Spanish for "hot waters", and the name meant what it said. Natural springs on the hill were spouting hot water at a temperature fairly close to boiling-point. But the springs were not the attraction for Ford and Fyfe. As geologists, they suspected from the shape of the hill that it stood on an oilfield, and they were right. Iquitos is now the very prosperous centre of a developing oil industry—although parts of the city still have rather a "backwoods" appearance, and a recent visitor has reported that vultures still wander through the streets scavenging.

In spite of its inland position, parts of Iquitos also have the air of a seaport, which in fact it is. As the terminus for ships coming up the Amazon from its mouth on the Atlantic Ocean 3,700 kilometres (2,300 miles) away, Iquitos is the furthest from the sea of all the world's ports.

Iquitos has about 200,000 people. The other towns of the Montaña are all much smaller—although several are developing quickly because of very serious attempts by the government to encourage settlers from the highlands, and so provide them with the chance to make a better living. These settlements are in areas that have been cleared of forest, and given road or river connections with local marketing centres. (The river connection is sometimes a raft of balsa logs lashed together in much the same way as the logs of the famous *Kon Tiki* were lashed.) Most of these towns also have road and air connections with Lima and the other large centres west of the Andes. The main town industries of such places are saw-milling and food-processing. The main farm crops are sugar-cane, coffee, tea, cocoa, rice, nuts, rubber, oil-palms, sweet potatoes and a variety of tropical fruits.

We have already met the Indians of the Montaña, but perhaps it should be added that the number of these people has grown much smaller since large-scale developments began in the nineteenth century. Many of them have now moved to remote areas that are unlikely to be reached by development. So it is still possible for adventurous visitors to find themselves among naked, painted people, hunting for their food with poisoned arrows and poisoned blowpipe darts. Nor, so Peruvians believe,

89

Yagua Indians, members of a primitive tribe who live in the Montaña region of Peru

is it impossible that some of the same painted people may still be cannibals.

The other inhabitants of the Montaña are, like the Peruvians of La Sierra and La Costa, mainly migrant highland Indians, *mestizos* or people whose ancestors were wholly Spanish. Nevertheless, there are some differences—for example, in parts of the "Eyebrow" there are communities of mainly fair-haired,

90

blue-eyed people. These are descendants of about seventy German and Austrian families who came to Peru around 1860. They cleared farms for themselves along a tributary of the Ucayali River, which is one of the streams which join to form the Amazon.

At the same time and after, migrants from a number of countries and continents came to work—and sometimes to settle permanently—in the Montaña. Their descendants, too, help to make Montaña people seem more of an international mixture than the Peruvians of La Sierra and La Costa. For this reason, and also because climate, vegetation, scenery and products are so different from those of the highlands and the coastlands, even western Peruvians sometimes feel that they are visiting a foreign country when they come east of the Andes.

Peru in the World

Modern Peru began its life as the senior Spanish colony in South America. It was the seat of the Viceroy, the Spanish king's representative. It was the base of the Spanish military and naval forces who were kept in South America to control warlike Indians, rebellious colonists and the British, French and Dutch pirates who often ravaged coastal settlements and captured Spanish cargo ships. It was the channel through which Spanish settlers everywhere on the continent were forced by law to export their products and import their needs. And, for at least two centuries, it was regarded as the centre of Spanish life and culture in the New World.

Perhaps because of those things, Peruvians of today sometimes seem inclined to think that their country has first place among the independent republics which were once Spanish colonies— but that remains to be proved. Since Peru became independent in 1824, its governments have been no more stable than any of the other South American governments, and much less stable than some. Nor has Peru been very successful in raising the extremely low living-standard of its large Indian population, in improving its farms and providing employment, or in achieving good relations with other South American republics. It has quarrelled with most of its neighbours and gone to war with three of them. A dispute which caused fighting with Ecuador as recently as 1981 has still not been settled.

However, it now seems that the future of Peru may be more stable, peaceful and successful than its past has been. Both inside and outside its boundaries, it has made much progress since the present democratically elected government took office in 1982. Also, Peru's position in world affairs has risen greatly since a Peruvian, Señor Javier Perez de Cuellar, became Secretary General of the United Nations Organization in 1982. Señor Perez de Cuellar took office shortly before the South American republic of Argentina attempted to take the Falkland Islands from Britain by force. His work during this very difficult time brought much credit to his country as well as to himself.

Within the American continents, Peru is now a member of the Latin American Integration Association (a ''common market'' agreement among eleven South and Central American countries). Peru has also joined some of its neighbours in a similar association of South American countries called the Andean Group, and is active in the Organization of American States, which is an attempt to make all the nations of both American continents work together for their own and each other's good.

Peru's place in all these organizations, and in the modern world generally, is becoming increasingly important. It will doubtless keep doing so while the country continues to have stable government free from the rebellions, military take-overs and violence which have caused so many setbacks in the past.

Index

Acari 18
Aguas Calientes 88
alpacas 9, 75
Altiplano 9
Amazonia *see* Montaña
Amazon, River 20, 86, 89, 91
anchoveta 56
Andean Group 93
Andes 7, 12, 13, 18, 20, 72, 84, 86
Anticona Pass 73
area of Peru 7
Arequipa 81-83
Argentina 7, 38, 93
Atahualpa 30, 34
Atlantic Ocean 20, 21, 32, 89
Ayacucho 40, 76-77
Aymará language 8

Balboa, Vasco Nuñez de 32
barriadas 51-52, 56, 59, 83
Bering Strait 21
Bolivar, Simon 39-40
Bolivia 9, 44
Brazil 7, 20

Cajamarca 33
caliche 44
Callao 16, 36, 40, 60, 81
Caribbean Sea 32
Central Line 72-74
Cerro de Pasco 53, 75
Chan-Chan 24
Chile 38, 44
Chimbote 55-56, 69, 72
Chimú empire 24, 25, 26
cinchona 88
climate 10, 11
coca 86-87
Cochrane, Admiral Lord 38
Columbus, Christopher 21, 32

communications 45, 89
conquistadores 35, 36, 88
constitution 46, 47
co-operative farms 58-59
Costa, La 7, 8, 13-18, 19, 61, 70
cotton 17, 45
criollos 36-37, 40, 41
Cuzco 22, 23, 24, 35, 78-79, 83

desert 7, 13-15

earthquakes 64-65, 66, 72, 78, 82
Ecuador 93
education 47-48
El Ciudad de los Reyes 62-63
El Dorado 33
El Misti 81
El Niño 15-16, 56, 61
Equator 7
European settlers 8, 9, 21, 22, 32, 36,
    88

farms, farming 9, 11, 13, 17, 19, 45,
    53, 56-59, 69, 74, 81-82, 89
fertilizer 17, 44
festivals 66-67, 80
fish, fishing 16, 17, 53, 55-56, 69
fishmeal 56, 69
flag 73
flooding 16
food 59, 69-70
forestry, forests 7, 19, 86

garúa 14
gold 29, 33, 86
government 46, 47
guano 17, 43-44

haciendas 57
handicrafts 75, 77

94

hats 77-78
Heyerdahl, Thor 80-81
Huancavelica 73, 74
Huancayo 74-75
Huascar 30, 34
Huayna Capac 29
Huayna Picchu 83
Humboldt current 14, 16, 17

Incas, Inca kingdom 22-30, 31, 80, 82, 83-85, 86
Inca remains (*see also* Cuzco *and* Machu Picchu) 70, 78-79, 83-85
independence, early days of 41-43
Indians, South American 8-9, 16, 19, 21, 57-58, 60, 80, 89-90
International Pacific Fair 68
Inti 25, 28, 31
Iquitos 20, 88-89
irrigation 17-18, 26, 81

Junin 40, 53
Junin, Lake 75

Kon Tiki 81

La Ceja de Montaña 85
Latin American Integration Association 93
La Oroya 75
latifundios 57
Lima 16, 35, 36, 37, 60, 61-68, 72
llamas 9, 75

Machu Picchu 83-85
manufacturing industry 45, 53, 55, 69, 83
Marcona 18
markets 75, 77, 80
maté 75, 77
medical care 50-51
mestizos 16, 37, 40, 41, 65, 90
mineral deposits, minerals 11, 19, 33, 53-54

miners, mining 9-10, 18, 45, 53-54, 74
Montaña, La 8, 13, 18-20, 54, 59-60, 68, 81, 83, 86-91
Mount Huascarán 72
Mount Meiggs 73

Nazca 70-71
nitrates 44

oases 16, 17, 68-69
oil, oilfields 18, 19, 54, 88
Organization of American States 93

Pacific Ocean 13, 22, 32, 61, 83
Panama 32, 35
Pan-American Highway 68
Pizarro, Francisco 32-33, 61, 62
population 8, 16, 19, 60, 61, 80, 83, 89
poverty 51-52, 59, 83, 92
Puerto Pizarro 32
Puno 79-80

Quechua Indians 8-9, 24
Quechua language 8, 22, 28

railways (*see also* Central Line) 45, 68, 72-74, 83
rainfall 13, 18, 84
Real Felipe 40
redistribution of land 58
Rimac 61-62, 63, 72
rivers 13, 17, 18
roads, Inca 27-28, 83, 86
roads, modern (*see also* Pan-American Highway) 45, 68
Rodil, José 40
Roman Catholic Church 48-50
rubber 88

Saint Martin de Porres 65
Saint Rose of Lima 65
San Martin, General 38-39
Santa, River 55, 72

Santo Domingo 65
Sapa Inca 25, 28, 29
Selva, La *see* Montaña, La
sheep 9
sicu 80
Sierra, La 8-13, 19, 68
silver 29, 33, 86
soroche 73
South America 7, 8, 20, 21
Spain, Spaniards 8, 32-37, 92
Spanish language 8
sport 67-68
Sucre, General Antonio 39-40
sugar cane 13, 17, 45

Tahuantinsuyo 28, 33
Talara 18, 54, 69

temperature 9, 13
Temple of the Sun 79
Titicaca, Lake 9, 24, 31, 79-81, 83
trees 12
Tropic of Capricorn 7
tropics 11-12
Trujillo 69
Tumbes 16

United Nations Organization 93
University of San Marcos 65
Uru Indians 80

War of the Pacific 44-45
West Indies 21
wildlife 16, 19-20